HALLOWEEN

Stories and Poems

Other collections by Caroline Feller Bauer

Rainy Day: *Stories and Poems*
Snowy Day: *Stories and Poems*
Windy Day: *Stories and Poems*

HALLOWEEN

Stories and Poems

Edited by Caroline Feller Bauer
Illustrated by Peter Sis

J.B. LIPPINCOTT

NEW YORK

Halloween: Stories and Poems
Text copyright © 1989 by Caroline Feller Bauer
Illustrations copyright © 1989 by Peter Sis
All rights reserved. No part of this book may be
used or reproduced in any manner whatsoever without
written permission except in the case of brief quotations
embodied in critical articles and reviews. Printed in
the United States of America. For information address
J. B. Lippincott Junior Books, 10 East 53rd Street,
New York, N.Y. 10022.
10 9 8 7 6 5 4 3 2

Library of Congress Cataloging-in-Publication Data
Halloween : stories and poems.

  Bibliography: p.
  Summary: A collection of Halloween stories and
poems by a variety of authors. Includes recipes and a
bibliography.
  1. Halloween—Literary collections. [1. Halloween—
Literary collections] I. Bauer, Caroline Feller.
II. Sis, Peter, ill.
PZ5.H157 1989   810'.8'033   88-2675
ISBN 0-397-32300-X
ISBN 0-397-32301-8 (lib. bdg.)

ACKNOWLEDGMENTS

Every effort has been made to trace ownership of all copyright material and to secure the necessary permissions to reprint these selections. In the event of any question arising as to the use of any material, the editor and the publisher, while expressing regret for any inadvertent error, will be happy to make the necessary correction in future printings. Thanks are due to the following for permission to reprint the copyrighted materials listed below:

Atheneum Publishers, a division of Macmillan, Inc., for "Night Scare" from *If I Were in Charge of the World and Other Worries*, by Judith Viorst. Copyright © 1981 Judith Viorst. / Nathalia Crane for "Spooks." / Curtis Brown, Ltd. for "Wicked Witch's Kitchen." Copyright © 1975 by X. J. Kennedy. / Farrar, Straus & Giroux, Inc. for "Pumpkin" from *More Small Poems* by Valerie Worth. Copyright © 1976 by Valerie Worth. / Susan Cohen Field for "The Princess and the Frog." / Robert Fisher for "I Once Dressed Up" from *Ghosts Galore*, edited by Robert Fisher, published by Faber and Faber Ltd. / Fontanna Young Lions, an imprint of the Collins Group, for "Ghosts" by Kit Wright. Copyright © 1978 by Kit Wright. / Greenwillow Books (A Division of William Morrow & Company) for "Ghost" from *It's Halloween!* by Jack Prelutsky. Copyright © 1977 by Jack Prelutsky. / Harper & Row, Publishers for "The Witch! The Witch!" from Eleanor Farjeon's *Poems for Children*. J. B. Lippincott. Copyright 1926, 1954 by Eleanor Farjeon. / Sharon Hudson for "Alone." / Julie Holder for "Scary Things" by Julie Holder, from *A Very First Poetry Book*, compiled by John Foster, published by Oxford University Press. / Houghton Mifflin Company for "King of the Cats" by Paul Galdone. Copyright © 1980 by Paul Galdone. / Instructor Publications, Inc. for "Halloween" by Phyllis J. Perry. Reprinted from *Instructor*, 1971. Copyright © 1971 by the Instructor Publications, Inc. Used by permission. / Daphne Lister for "Under the Stairs" from *Gingerbread Pigs & Other Rhymes*, published by Transworld Ltd., Corgi-Carousel. / McIntosh and Otis, Inc. and Michael Patrick Hearn for "Curses." Copyright © 1979 by Michael Patrick Hearn. / Oxford University Press for "Forbidden Sounds" by Eric James. Reprinted from *Ghosts, Witches and Things Like That* edited by Roderick Hunt (1984). Copyright © 1984 Oxford University Press. / Jane Pridmore for "In the Dark." / The James Reeves Estate for "The Bogus-Boo." Copyright © James Reeves. / Marian Reiner for The Estate of Harry Behn for "Ghosts" from *The Golden Hive Poems and Pictures* by Harry Behn. Copyright © 1957, 1962, 1966 by Harry Behn. All rights reserved. / Marian Reiner for "Fog" and "I'm Skeleton." Copyright © 1975 by Lilian Moore. All rights reserved. / Scholastic Inc. for "The Haunted House" by Vic Crume, from *Haunted House and Other Spooky Poems and Tales* edited by Gladys Schwartz and Vic Crume. Copyright © 1970 by Scholastic Magazines, Inc. / Scholastic Inc. for "The Bed Just So" by Jeanne B. Hardendorff. Copyright © 1975 by Jeanne B. Hardendorff. / Scholastic Inc. for "The Jigsaw Puzzle" from *The Tales for the Midnight Hour* by Judith Bauer Stamper. Copyright © 1977 by Judith Bauer Stamper. / Scholastic Inc. for "Something Is There" from *Spooky Rhymes and Riddles* by Lilian Moore. Copyright © 1972 by Lilian Moore. / Ian Serraillier for "The Visitor." Copyright © 1980 Ian Serraillier and Oxford University Press. / Grace Cornell Tall for "Hallowe'en Ad" and for "To Pumpkins at Pumpkin Time."

FOR PETER
who never tricks
but always treats

Contents

HALLOWEEN

Stories and Poems

King of the Cats

A Ghost Story by JOSEPH JACOBS
Retold by PAUL GALDONE

One October evening the gravedigger's wife was sitting by the fireside with her big black cat, Old Tom. They were waiting for the gravedigger to come home.

They waited and waited, but still he didn't come.

At last he came rushing in, and as he came he called, "Who's Tom Tildrum?"

He said it in such a wild way that both his wife and his cat stared at him in fright.

"Why, what's the matter?" said his wife. "And why do you want to know who Tom Tildrum is?"

"I was digging away at Old Mr. Fordyce's grave when I suppose I must have dropped asleep. I only woke up when I heard a cat's 'miaow.'"

"Miaow," said Old Tom in answer.

"Yes, just like that!" said the gravedigger. "So I looked over the edge of the grave, and what do you think I saw?"

"Now, how can I tell?" said his wife.

"Why, nine black cats, all like our friend Tom here. All of them had white spots on their chests, and what do you think they were carrying? Why, a small coffin covered with a velvet pall. On the pall was a small coronet of gold, and at every third step they took they cried all together, 'Miaow.'"

"Miaow!" said Old Tom again.

"Yes, just like that!" said the gravedigger. "And as they came nearer and nearer to me, I could see them more distinctly because their eyes shone with a sort of green light. The biggest cat of all was walking in front. And he looked for all the world like . . ."

Suddenly the gravedigger stopped talking.

"Just look at our Tom, how he's looking at me," the gravedigger said. "You'd think he knew all I was saying."

"Go on, go on," said his wife. "Never mind Old Tom."

4

"Well, as I was a-saying, the nine cats came toward me slowly and solemnly. And at every third step they all cried together—"

"Miaow!" said Old Tom again.

"Yes, just like that," said the gravedigger. "The cats came on and on till they stood right opposite Mr. Fordyce's grave, where I was. Then they all stood still and looked straight at me. I did feel queer, that I did!

"But look at Old Tom," said the gravedigger. He's looking at me just like they did."

"Go on, go on," said his wife. "Never mind Old Tom."

"Where was I?!" said the gravedigger. "Oh yes. There they all stood, still looking at me, when the one that wasn't carrying the coffin came forward. Staring straight at me, he said to me—yes, I tell you, he *said* to me, in a squeaky voice, 'TELL TOM TILDRUM THAT TIM TILDRUM'S DEAD.'

"And that's why I asked if you knew who Tom Tildrum was, for how can I tell Tom Tildrum that Tim Tildrum's dead if I don't know who Tom Tildrum is?"

"Look at Old Tom, look at Old Tom!" screamed the gravedigger's wife. And well he might look, for Tom was swelling and Tom was staring and at last Tom shrieked out:

"What—old Tim dead? Then I, Tom Tildrum, am King of the Cats!"

And Old Tom rushed up the chimney and was never seen again.

Halloween

PHYLLIS J. PERRY

Hooting
  Howling
    Hissing
      Witches

Riding
  Rasping
    Ragged
      Switches;

Fluttering
  Frightening
    Fearsome
      Bats;

Arching
  Awesome
    Awful
      Cats;

Long
   Lantern-
      Lighted
       Streets;

Tricks!
  Tasty
    Tempting
     Treats!

To Pumpkins
at Pumpkin Time

GRACE TALL

Back into your garden-beds!
  Here come the holidays!
And woe to the golden pumpkin-heads
  Attracting too much praise.
Hide behind the hoe, the plow,
  Cling fast to the vine!
Those who come to praise you now
  Will soon sit down to dine.
Keep your lovely heads, my dears,
  If you know what I mean . . .
Unless you sigh to be in pie,
  Stay hidden, or stay green.

Alone

SHARON HUDSON

Alone in a house with no one to talk to,
With the floorboards squeaking,
And the wall boards creaking,
Windows rattling like ghost tapping.

Rustling trees, knocking knees,
Scaredly I walk down the hall;
Footsteps following I call,
No one answers, no one at all.

Ghosts

KIT WRIGHT

That's right. Sit down and talk to me.
What do you want to talk about?

Ghosts. You were saying that you believe in them.
Yes, they exist, without a doubt.

What, bony white nightmares that rattle and glow?
No, just spirits that come and go.

I've never heard such a load of rubbish.
Never mind, one day you'll know.

What makes you so sure?

I said:
What makes you so sure?

Hey,
Where did you go?

The Princess and the Frog

SUSAN COHEN FIELD

A princess kissed a frog one day
And much to her surprise,
It turned into a fat, old witch
Right before her eyes!

I'm Skeleton

LILIAN MOORE

I'm the local Skeleton
who walks this
street.
This is my beat.
Beware!
I'm not very hairy
but I scare
everyone I meet.

People quiver
when they see me.
They flee me!
They shiver
if they must walk
alone.

Oops, there's a dog.
I must run.
His tail has a wag.
He wants to play tag.
And how he would like a
bone!

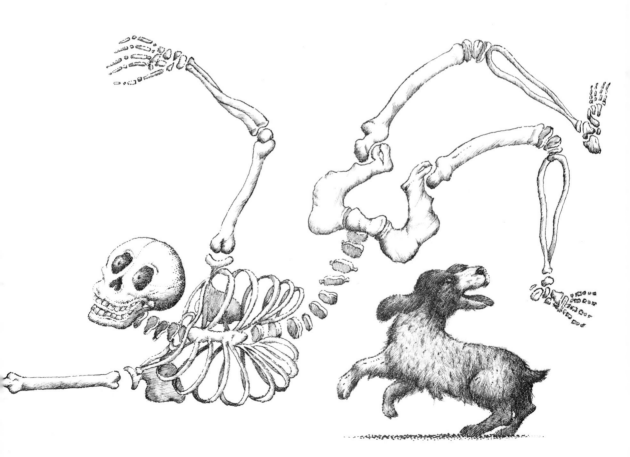

Forbidden Sounds

ERIC JAMES

When the banshees wail,
And the werewolves howl,
When the dead in the churchyard sigh.
When the witches scream,
And their demons hiss,
When you hear the song of the Lorelei.
When the bogies shout,
And when goblins yell.
When the shades call out
From the depths of Hell.
When the phantom drummer
Drums his drum,
When the midnight wraith
Whispers, "Come, oh come . . ."
Then who will go?

Not I.

The Witch! The Witch!

ELEANOR FARJEON

The Witch! The Witch!
Don't let her get you!
Or your Aunt wouldn't know you
    the next time she met you!

I Once Dressed Up

ROBERT FISHER

I once dressed up as a ghost
It was wet and I was bored
Waiting for Mum to come home
Drawing pictures on the windows
And chewing a bit of cheese
Then it hit me—this idea
So I got an old sheet from the airing cupboard
I was only six at the time or seven
And put it over my head
Couldn't see couldn't hear anything
Except the sound of breathing
The world went white then black
I waited
A lonely ghost by the stairs
Then I heard a bang and the sound
  of f-o-o-t-s-t-e-p-s
    coming closer
"Hellooooo," said a creepy voice
I shot out from that sheet double quick

The sheet was white and so was I
"It's only me," I said
Mum laughed
It can be quite scary being a ghost

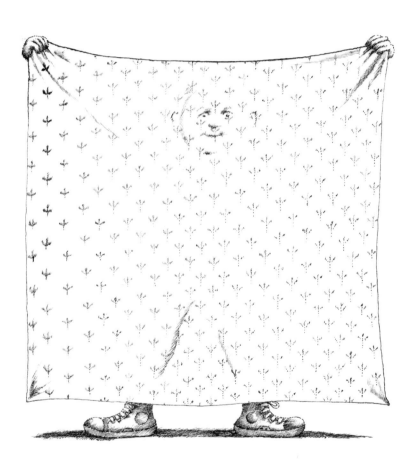

The Hairy Toe

ANONYMOUS

Once there was a woman went out to pick beans,
and she found a Hairy Toe.
She took the Hairy Toe home with her,
and that night, when she went to bed,
the wind began to moan and groan.
Away off in the distance
she seemed to hear a voice crying,
"Where's my Hair-r-ry To-o-oe?
Who's got my Hair-r-ry To-o-oe?"

The woman scrooched down,
'way down under the covers,
and about that time
the wind appeared to hit the house,

smoosh,

and the old house creaked and cracked
like something was trying to get in.
The voice had come nearer,
almost at the door now,

and it said,
"Where's my Hair-r-ry To-o-oe?
Who's got my Hair-r-ry To-o-oe?"

The woman scrooched further down
under the covers
and pulled them tight around her head.

The wind growled around the house
like some big animal
and r-r-um-umbled
over the chimney.
All at once she heard the door cr-r-a-ack
and Something slipped in
and began to creep over the floor.

The floor went
cre-e-eak, cre-e-eak
at every step that thing took toward her bed.
The woman could almost feel it bending over her head.
There in an awful voice it said:
"Where's my Hair-r-ry To-o-oe?
Who's got my Hair-r-ry To-o-oe?
You've got it!"

Epitaphs

Why not try to write your own gravestone epitaph?

Here lies
Uncle George
Aged 104
"The Good Die
Young"

•

So died John So.
So, so, did he so?
So did he live
And so did he die.
So, so did he so,
And so let him lie.

•

Here lies the body of our Anna
Done to death by a banana.
It wasn't the fruit that laid her low
But the skin of the thing that made her go.

Underneath this pile of stones
Lies all that's left of Sally Jones.
Her name was Briggs, it was not Jones,
But Jones was used to rhyme with stones.

●

Beneath this stone, a lump of clay,
Lies Uncle Peter Daniels,
Who too early in the month of May
Took off his winter flannels.

●

One fine day in the middle of the night
Two dead men got up to fight.
Back to back they faced each other,
Drew their swords and shot each other.

●

It was a cough
    that carried her off,
It was a coffin
    they carried her off in.

The Jigsaw Puzzle

J. B. STAMPER

It was on the top shelf of an old bookcase, covered with dust and barely visible. Lisa decided she had to find out what it was. Of all the things in the old junk shop, it aroused her curiosity most. She had looked through old books, prints, and postcards for years. Nothing had caught her interest. Now the old box, high and out of reach, intrigued her.

She looked around for the old man who ran the store. But he had gone into the back room. She saw a stepladder across the room and brought it over to the bookcase. It shook on the uneven floorboards as she climbed to the top step.

Lisa patted her hand along the surface of the top shelf, trying to find the box. The dirt was thick and gritty on the board. Then she touched the box. It was made of cardboard. The cardboard was cold and soft from being in the damp room for such a long time. She lifted the box slowly, trying to steady her balance on the stepladder.

As the side of the box reached her eye level, she could read the words:

500 PIECES

She sat the box down on top of the stepladder and climbed down a few steps. Then she blew away some of the dust that had accumulated on the lid. It billowed up around her with a musty, dead odor. But now she could make out a few more words on top of the box:

THE STRANGEST
JIGSAW PUZZLE
IN THE WORLD

There were other words underneath that, but they had been rubbed off the cardboard lid. The big picture on the cover had been curiously damaged. Lisa could make out areas of light and dark. It looked as though the scene might be in a room. But most of the picture had been scratched off the cardboard box, probably by a sharp instrument.

The mysterious nature of the jigsaw puzzle made it even more appealing to Lisa. She decided she would buy it. The lid was taped down securely; that probably meant that all the pieces would be there. As she carefully climbed down the stepladder, holding the box in both hands, Lisa smiled to herself. It was quite a find, just the sort of thing she had always hoped to discover while rummaging through secondhand stores.

Mr. Tuborg, the owner of the store, came out of the back room as she was walking up to his sales desk. He looked curiously at the box when Lisa set it down.

"And where did you find that?" he asked her.

Lisa pointed to where she had set up the stepladder. "It was on top of that bookcase. You could barely see it from the floor."

"Well, I've never seen it before, that's for sure," Mr. Tuborg said. "Can't imagine how you found it."

Lisa was more pleased than ever about her find. She felt as though the puzzle had been hiding up there, waiting for her to discover it. She paid Mr. Tuborg the twenty-five cents he asked for the puzzle and then wrapped it carefully in the newspapers he gave her to take it home in.

As soon as she had climbed the flight of stairs to her room, Lisa cleaned off the big table in the center of the room. She set the box down on it.

THE STRANGEST
JIGSAW PUZZLE
IN THE WORLD

Lisa read the words again. She wondered what they could mean. How strange could a jigsaw puzzle be?

The tape that held the lid down was still strong. Lisa got out a kitchen knife to slice through it. When she lifted the cover off the box, a musty smell came from inside. But the jigsaw pieces all looked in good condition. Lisa picked one up. The color was faded, but the picture was clear. She could see the shape of a finger in the piece. It looked like a woman's finger.

Lisa sat down and started to lay out the pieces, topside up, on the large table. As she took them from the box, she sorted out the flat-edged pieces from the inside pieces. Every so often, she would recognize something in one of the pieces. She saw some blond hair, a windowpane, and a small vase. There was a lot of wood texture in the pieces, plus what looked like wallpaper. Lisa noticed that the wallpaper in the puzzle looked a lot like the wallpaper in her own room. She wondered if her wallpaper was as old as the jigsaw puzzle. It would be an incredible coincidence, but it could be the same.

By the time Lisa had all the pieces laid out on the table, it was 6:30. She got up and made herself a sandwich. Already, her back was beginning to hurt a little from leaning over the table. But she couldn't stay away from the puzzle. She went back to the table and set her sandwich down beside her. It was always like that when she did jigsaws. Once she started, she couldn't stop until the puzzle was all put together.

She began to sort out the edge pieces according to their coloring. There were dark brown pieces, whitish pieces, the wallpaper pieces, and some pieces that seemed to be like glass—perhaps a window. As she slowly ate her sandwich, Lisa pieced together the border. When she was finished, she knew she had been right about the setting of the picture when she had first seen the puzzle. It was a room. One side of the border was wallpaper. Lisa decided to fill that in first. She was curious about its resemblance to her own wallpaper.

29

She gathered all the pieces together that had the blue and lilac flowered design. As she fit the pieces together, it became clear that the wallpaper in the puzzle was identical to the wallpaper in her room. Lisa glanced back and forth between the puzzle and her wall. It was an exact match.

By now it was 8:30. Lisa leaned back in her chair. Her back was stiff. She looked over at her window. The night was black outside. Lisa got up and walked over to the window. Suddenly, she felt uneasy, alone in the apartment. She pulled the white shade over the window.

She paced around the room once, trying to think of something else she might do other than finish the puzzle. But nothing else interested her. She went back and sat down at the table.

Next she started to fill in the lower right-hand corner. There was a rug and then a chair. This part of the puzzle was very dark. Lisa noticed uneasily that the chair was the same shape as one sitting in the corner of her room. But the colors didn't seem exactly the same. Her chair was maroon. The one in the puzzle was in the shadows and seemed almost black.

Lisa continued to fill in the border toward the middle. There was more wallpaper to finish on top. The left-hand side did turn out to be a window. Through it, a half moon hung in a dark sky. But it was the bottom on the puzzle that began to bother Lisa. As the pieces fell into place, she saw a picture of a pair of legs, crossed underneath a table. They were the legs of a young woman. Lisa reached down and ran her hand along one of her legs. Suddenly, she had felt as though something was crawling up it, but it must have been her imagination.

She stared down at the puzzle. It was almost three quarters done. Only the middle remained. Lisa glanced at the lid to the puzzle box:

THE STRANGEST
JIGSAW . . .

She shuddered.

Lisa leaned back in her chair again. Her back ached. Her neck muscles were tense and strained. She thought about quitting the puzzle. It scared her now.

She stood up and stretched. Then she looked down at the puzzle on the table. It looked different from the higher angle. Lisa was shocked by what she saw. Her body began to tremble all over.

It was unmistakable—the picture in the puzzle was of her own room. The window was placed correctly in relation to the table. The bookcase stood in its exact spot against the wall. Even the carved table legs were the same. . . .

Lisa raised her hand to knock the pieces of the puzzle apart. She didn't want to finish the strangest jigsaw puzzle in the world; she didn't want to find out what the hole in the middle of the puzzle might turn out to be.

But then she lowered her hand. Perhaps it was worse not to know. Perhaps it was worse to wait and wonder.

Lisa sank back down into the chair at the table. She fought off the fear that crept into the sore muscles on her back. Deliberately, piece by piece, she began to fill in the hole in the puzzle. She put together a picture of a table, on which lay a jigsaw puzzle. This puzzle inside the puzzle was finished. But Lisa couldn't make out what it showed. She pieced together the young woman who was herself. As she filled in the picture, her own body slowly filled with horror and dread. It was all there in the picture . . . the vase filled with blue cornflowers, her red cardigan sweater, the wild look of fear in her own face.

33

The jigsaw puzzle lay before her—finished except for two adjoining pieces. They were dark pieces, ones she hadn't been able to fit into the area of the window. Lisa looked behind her. The white blind was drawn over her window. With relief, she realized that the puzzle picture was not exactly like her room. It showed the black night behind the window pane and a moon shining in the sky.

With trembling hands, Lisa reached for the second to last piece. She dropped it into one of the empty spaces. It seemed to be half a face, but not a human face. She reached for the last piece. She pressed it into the small hole left in the picture.

The face was complete—the face in the window. It was more horrible than anything she had ever seen, or dreamed. Lisa looked at the picture of herself in the puzzle and then back to that face.

Then she whirled around. The blind was no longer over her window. The night showed black through the windowpane. A half moon hung low in the sky.

Lisa screamed. . . . The face . . . it was there, too.

35

The Haunted House

VIC CRUME

Not a window was broken
And the paint wasn't peeling,
  Not a porch step sagged—
  Yet, there was a feeling

That beyond the door
And into the hall
  This was the house of
  No one at all.

No one who breathed
Nor laughed, nor ate
  Nor said "I love,"
  Nor said "I hate."

Yet *something* walked
Along the stair
  Something that was
  And wasn't there.

And that is why weeds
On the path grow high,
  And even the moon
  Races fearfully by—

For *something* walks
Along the stair—
  Something that is
  And isn't there.

Pumpkin

VALERIE WORTH

After its lid
Is cut, the slick
Seeds and stuck
Wet strings
Scooped out,
Walls scraped
Dry and white,
Face carved, candle
Fixed and lit,

Light creeps
Into the thick
Rind: giving
That dead orange
Vegetable skull
Warm skin, making
A live head
To hold its
Sharp gold grin.

In the Dark

JANE PRIDMORE

A man runs across the ceiling
Of my bedroom,
Someone with long hands patterned with leaves.

The wardrobe looks like a huge bird,
Six times bigger than an eagle.
I don't like the dark.

The flowers on the table near the window
Catch the street light as it shines on them
Then they look like little heads.

When the wind blows it comes through the door,
And to me it sounds like a ghost
Worming its way through the cracks.
At night everything looks different
All sorts of ghostly shapes
In the dark.

Curses!

MICHAEL PATRICK HEARN

First Witch:

Ragwort, tansy, parsley, pea!
 You'd better stay away from me!
Purple pumpkins, crabgrass green!
 You're the ugliest thing I've ever seen!
Bumble,
Grumble,
Mumblety peg!
Let a worm crawl up your leg!
Brooklyn needle,
Jersey pin!
Let a snail sit on your chin!
 Nyeh!

40

Curses!

Second Witch:

Oh, pickle water!
Penguin toes!
Let your nose grow like a gardenia grows!
Six times six,
And two times two!
    Let your hair turn blue!
    Let your hair turn blue!
    Let it stick like glue!
And if you think that's bad,
    If you think that's bad,
    If you think *that's* bad,
Here's something worse:
You'll never get free of *my* witch's curse!
    So there!

Wicked Witch's Kitchen

X. J. KENNEDY

You're in the mood for freaky food?
You feel your taste buds itchin'
For nice fresh poison ivy greens?
Try Wicked Witch's kitchen!

She has corn on the cobweb, cauldron-hot,
She makes the meanest cider,
But her broomstick cakes and milkweed shakes
Aren't fit to feed a spider.

She likes to brew hot toadstool stew—
"Come eat, my sweet!" she'll cackle—
But if you do, you'll turn into
A jack-o'-lantern's jackal.

Ghosts

HARRY BEHN

A cold and starry darkness moans
   And settles wide and still
Over a jumble of tumbled stones
   Dark on a darker hill.

An owl among those shadowy walls,
   Gray against the gray
Of ruins and brittle weeds, calls
   And soundless swoops away.

Rustling over scattered stones
   Dancers hover and sway,
Drifting among their own bones
   Like webs of the Milky Way.

Fog

LILIAN MOORE

Oh this is
Witches' Weather—
swirling
misting—
Oh this is
Witches' Weather
so don't go out
today!

They'll
wrap you round
in cobwebs—
curling
twisting—
They'll
wrap you round
in cobwebs
and you'll
never
find your
way!

Halloo!
Halloo!
I'm here.

Where are *you*?

The Bogus-Boo

JAMES REEVES

The Bogus-boo
Is a creature who
Comes out at night—and why?
He likes the air;
He likes to scare
The nervous passer-by.

Out from the park
At dead of dark
He comes with huffling pad.
If, when alone,
You hear his moan
'Tis like to drive you mad.

He has two wings,
Pathetic things,
With which he cannot fly.
His tusks look fierce,
Yet could not pierce
The merest butterfly.

He has six ears,
But what he hears
Is very faint and small;
And with the claws
On his eight paws
He cannot scratch at all.

He looks so wise
With his owl-eyes,
His aspect grim and ghoulish,
But truth to tell
He sees not well
And is distinctly foolish.

This Bogus-boo
What can he do
But huffle in the dark?
So don't take fright;
He has no bite
And very little bark.

Spider on the Floor

ANONYMOUS

There's a spider on the floor
There's a spider on the floor
There's a spider on the floor
There's a spider on the floor
Who could ask for more
Than a spider on the floor
There's a spider on the floor
There's a spider on the floor.

Now the spider's on my leg
He's really, really big
This old spider on my leg
Oh, there's a spider on my leg.

Now the spider's on my stomach
Oh, he's just a big old lummock
This old spider on my stomach
There's a spider on my stomach.

Now the spider's on my neck
Oh, I'm gonna be a wreck
There's a spider on my neck

Now the spider's on my face
Oh, what a big disgrace
There's a spider on my face

Now the spider's on my head
Oh, I wish that I were dead
There's a spider on my head

But he jumps off
        Prrrrrrrrr—Pop!

Now there's a spider on the floor
Now there's a spider on the floor
Now there's a spider on the floor
Now there's a spider on the floor
Who could ask for anything more
Than a spider on the floor
There's a spider on the floor
There's a spider on the floor.

Ghostly Antidotes

When you are getting ready for bed, place one shoe with the toe pointing under the bed. Place the other shoe pointing in the opposite direction. Now you will be safe from ghosts and goblins throughout the night.

Keep ghosts away. Turn your pockets inside out.

Carry a piece of bread crust in your pocket. It will protect you from creatures that roam in the night.

You can also get rid of a ghost by throwing a key at it.

If you should meet a witch, cross your fingers and you'll stay safe.

Hang a mirror on the front porch. It will keep ghosts from coming into your house.

At the first light of day ghosts, goblins, witches, and zombies disappear.

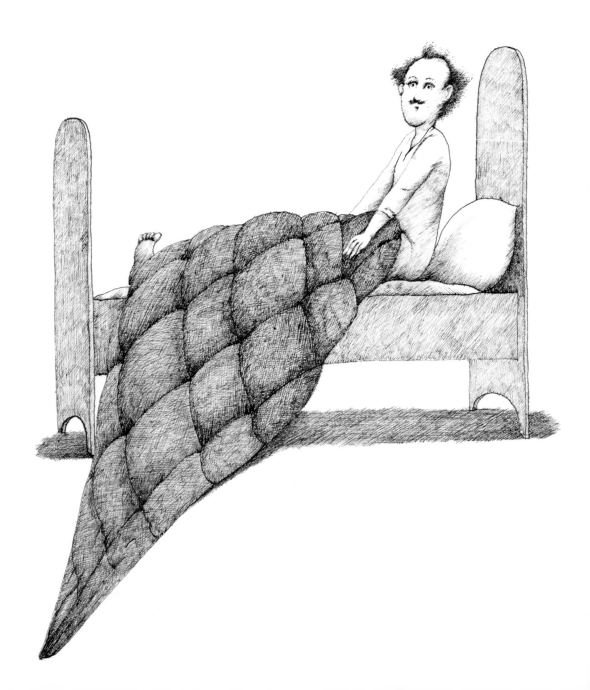

The Bed Just So

Retold by JEANNE B. HARDENDORFF

Once there was a tailor who fell asleep over his work every day. He was sleepy all day long . . . because he could not get any sleep at night.

Every night, when he began to fall asleep, someone—or some*thing*—pulled the covers off his bed. And all night long, the tailor thought he heard someone or some*thing* grumbling and complaining and stomping around. "This can't go on," the tailor said. And he went to see the Wise Woman.

"I must be witched," he told her.

"No," the Wise Woman said. "If you were witched,

your feet would be on backwards. And your hair would be growing upside down. No. Your trouble is that a hudgin has come to stay with you."

"A hudgin!" said the tailor. "What should I do?"

"Make a bed for him," the Wise Woman said. "Then he will leave your bed alone."

So the tailor bought a bed for the hudgin. It was a big, high bed made of oak wood.

"Now," said the tailor, "you have your bed and I have mine. Let's both have a good night's sleep."

But as soon as the tailor began to fall asleep, he heard a voice grumbling and complaining:

Too high and too hard!

Too high and too hard!

The next night, the tailor made a low bed of fern and feathers.

But as soon as he began to fall asleep, a voice woke him up, grumbling and complaining:

Too soft and too tickly!

Too soft and too tickly!

Every day the tailor tried a new bed for the hudgin. Every night the voice woke him up, grumbling and complaining.

When the tailor made a bed in the cupboard, the voice said:

Too dark and too stuffy!

Too dark and too stuffy!

Then he tried a hammock. But the voice said:

Too long and too loose!

Too long and too loose!

The tailor built a cradle. The voice complained:

Too teeter and too totter!

Too teeter and too totter!

The poor tailor could not find a bed to please the hudgin. "I will never get a good night's sleep," thought the tailor. He was very, very tired.

But that night he cracked open a walnut to eat after dinner. He looked at the half walnut shell, and it looked to him like a tiny bed.

"Why not?" the tailor thought. "I have tried everything else."

So he lined the walnut shell with cotton and peach down. He put a maple leaf on for a cover. And he put it on the windowsill.

Soon he heard a happy humming sound. The tailor looked in the walnut shell. There he saw a small dot, no bigger than a mustard seed.

"Ah, that must be the hudgin," said the tailor. He shut his eyes tight to listen. And he heard a contented voice saying:

"Just so. Just so.

I like a bed made just so."

And at last the tailor got a good night's sleep.

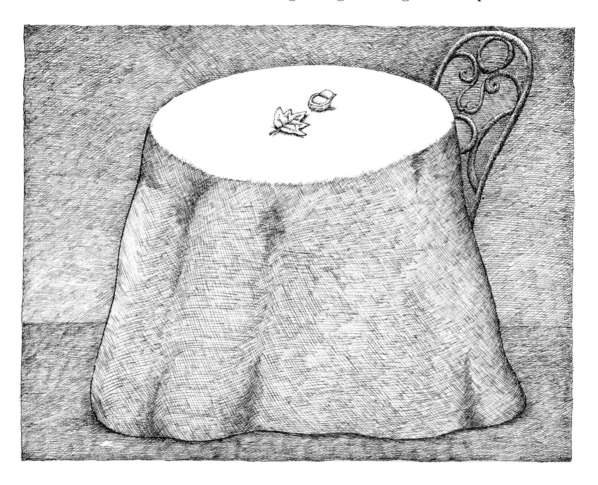

Scary Things

JULIE HOLDER

Under the bed
After saying goodnight,
Getting stuck in a sweater
That's much too tight,
Getting lost at the fair
or the shops or the zoo,
Feeling something
With lots of legs
Crawling on you.

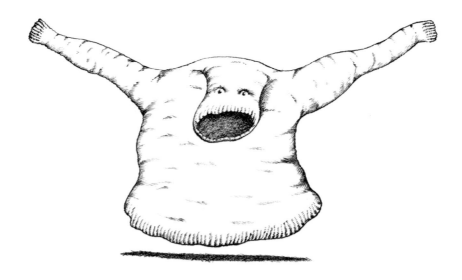

Something Is There

LILIAN MOORE

Something is there
  there on the stair
    coming down
      coming down
        stepping with care.
      Coming down
        coming down
        slinkety-sly

Something is coming and wants to get by.

Ghost

JACK PRELUTSKY

I saw a ghost
   that stared and stared
And I stood still
   and acted scared.
But that was just
   a big pretend.

I knew that ghost . . .

. . . it was my friend!

Night Scare

JUDITH VIORST

There aren't any ghosts.
There aren't any.
There aren't any gho—
Well . . . not too many.

Hallowe'en Ad
(Attention, Witches!)

GRACE TALL

I've no bat for your witchcraft,
No owl, no mouse,
But I do have a spider
That's new in my house,
'e's little and dark
And a wee bit stout,
And I don't have the heart
To put him out.
If you need a spider
For your witchery,
Contact the writer,
You can have him free.

Under the Stairs

DAPHNE LISTER

I don't like the cupboard
Under the stairs,
It reminds me of caves
And dragons' lairs.

So I never look in
Once it is night,
In case I should get
A nasty fright.

I'm silly I know,
'Cos it's only small,
There wouldn't be room
For a dragon, at all.

But even in daytime
It gives me the scares
To go past the cupboard
Under the stairs.

63

Spooks

NATHALIA CRANE

Oh, I went down to Framingham
  To sit on a graveyard wall;
"If there be spooks," I said to myself,
  "I shall see them, one and all."

I hugged the knee to still the heart,
  My gaze on a tomb 'neath a tree.
Down in the village the clock struck nine,
  But never a ghost did I see.

A boy passed by, and his hair was red;
  He paused by a sunken mound.
"How goes it with all the ghosts?" said he.
  "Have you heard any walking around?"

Now the taunt was the sign of a boy's disdain
  For the study I did pursue.
So I took the hour to teach that lad
  Of the things unseen but true.

And suddenly a bat swung by,
   Two cats began to bawl,
And that red-haired boy walked off in haste
   When I needed him most of all.

I lost a slipper as I fled—
   I bumped against a post;
But nevertheless I knew I'd won
   The secret of raising a ghost.

And the method is this—at least for a miss—
   You must sit on a graveyard wall,
And talk of the things you never have seen,
   And you'll see them, one and all.

The Visitor

IAN SERRAILLIER

A crumbling churchyard, the sea.and the moon;
The waves had gouged out grave and bone;
A man was walking, late and alone. . . .

He saw a skeleton on the ground;
A ring on a bony hand he found.

He ran home to his wife and gave her the ring.
"Oh, where did you get it?" He said not a thing.

"It's the prettiest ring in the world," she said,
As it glowed on her finger. They skipped off to bed.

At midnight they woke. In the dark outside—
"Give me my ring!" a chill voice cried.

"What was that, William? What did it say?"
"Don't worry, my dear. It'll soon go away."

"I'm coming!" A skeleton opened the door.
"Give me my ring!" It was crossing the floor.

"What was that, William? What did it say?"
"Don't worry, my dear. It'll soon go away."

"I'm touching you now! I'm climbing the bed."
The wife pulled the sheet right over her head.

It was torn from her grasp and tossed in the air:
"I'll drag you out of your bed by the hair!"

"What was that, William? What did it say?"
"Throw the ring through the window!

THROW IT AWAY!"

She threw it. The skeleton leapt from the sill,
Scooped up the ring and clattered downhill,
Fainter . . . and fainter. . . . Then all was still.

GHOSTLY COOKIES

You need:

> ½ cup wheat germ
> 1½ cups peanut butter
> 1½ cups honey
> 3 cups powdered milk
> ¾ cup graham cracker crumbs
> powdered sugar

To make:

Mix together the first five ingredients. Roll into small balls and then coat with powdered sugar. This recipe makes about five dozen cookies.

GOBLIN'S FLOAT

You need:

> 1 gallon apple cider
> 2 quarts vanilla ice cream
> Nutmeg

To make:

Chill the cider. When chilled, pour the cider into tall glasses, but fill only partway. Add two scoops ice cream to each glass, then add a dash of nutmeg to the top of the ice cream.

WITCHES' BREW

You need:

> 2 6-oz. cans frozen lemonade concentrate
> 2 quarts apple juice
> 2 quarts ginger ale
> 2 cups orange juice
> lemon slices

Combine all ingredients and chill. Then pour the witches' brew over ice cubes in tall glasses. Float a lemon slice in each glass.

69

Read About Halloween

Index

Read About Halloween

PICTURE BOOKS

Haunted House by Jan Pienkowski. Illustrated by the author. Dutton. A fabulous pop-up book is a tour of a haunted house.

It Hardly Seems Like Halloween by David S. Rose. Lothrop. Although a small boy is surrounded by ghosts and witches, he thinks "there's not an eerie creature to be seen."

Scary, Scary Halloween by Eve Bunting. Illustrated by Jan Breet. Clarion. "Trick or treat? It's Halloween! Am I the scariest thing you've seen?"

Space Case by Edward Marshall. Illustrated by James Marshall. Dial. A thing from outer space arrives on Halloween night.

Teeny Tiny by Jill Bennett. Illustrated by Tomie de Paola. Putnam. A teeny tiny woman finds a teeny tiny bone on a teeny tiny grave. The owner wants it back.

The Biggest Pumpkin Ever by Steven Kroll. Illustrated by Jeri Bassett. Holiday. Two mice tend a pumpkin that grows and grows.

73

The Ghost-Eye Tree by Bill Martin, Jr., and John Archambault. Illustrated by Ted Rand. Holt, Rinehart and Winston. How dark it was, how dread it was, "as a little boy and his big sister approached the Ghost-Eye Tree."

The Little Old Lady Who Was Not Afraid of Anything by Linda Williams. Illustrated by Megan Lloyd. Crowell. Clomp, Clomp. Shake, Shake. Nod, Nod. The little old lady is chased through the dark woods by some noisy clothes and a pumpkin head.

The Vanishing Pumpkin by Tony Johnston. Illustrated by Tomie de Paola. Putnam. "Our pumpkin's been snitched," cries the 700-year-old man, and searches for it with an 800-year-old man.

The Witch Who Lives Down the Hall by Donna Guthrie. Illustrated by Amy Schwartz. Harcourt. Witches love Halloween. Is Ms. McWee a witch?

LONGER BOOKS

America's Very Own Ghosts by Daniel Cohen. Illustrated by Alix Berenzy. Dodd, Mead. Short stories about some famous American ghosts.

"Night of the Jack-O'-Lantern" in *Ramona and Her Father*. Illustrated by Alan Tiegreen. Morrow. Picky-Picky eats the "wickedest jack-o'-lantern in the whole world."

The Ghosts of Austwich Manor by Reby Edmond MacDonald. McElderry/Atheneum. Hillary and Heather try to save their brother from the curse of an old Tudor house.

The Princess and the Goblin by George MacDonald. Illustrated by Jessie Willcox Smith. Morrow. Princess Irene and her friend Curdie meet the goblins beneath the castle.

The Wednesday Witch by Ruth Chew. Illustrated by the author. Scholastic. Mary Jane meets a short, fat woman who wears a black dress and a pointed hat.

The Witches by Roald Dahl. Illustrated by Quentin Blake. Farrar, Straus. A young boy attends a meeting of witches and even meets The Grand High Witch.

"Treats and Tricks" in *Nora and Mrs. Mind Your Own Business* by Johanna Hurwitz. Illustrated by Susan Jeschke. Morrow. Nora and Teddy give treats instead of asking for them one Halloween night.

Uninvited Ghosts by Penelope Lively. Illustrated by John Lawrence. Dutton. What happens when a ghost oozes out of a dresser drawer.

What's Happened to Harry? by Barbara Dillon. Illustrated by Chris Conover. Morrow. Harry meets a witch and is turned into a dog.

Witch-Cat by Joan Carris. Illustrated by Beth Peck. Lippincott. Witch-cat is assigned to Gwen, a little girl who doesn't believe in magic.

Index

Recognized for her combined skills as author, lecturer, teacher, educational consultant, and librarian, CAROLINE FELLER BAUER travels frequently, lecturing most often on her favorite subject—bringing children and books together.

She is the author of MY MOM TRAVELS A LOT, TOO MANY BOOKS!, and THIS WAY TO BOOKS. She is the editor of CELEBRATIONS, PRESENTING READER'S THEATER, as well as RAINY DAY: STORIES AND POEMS, SNOWY DAY: STORIES AND POEMS, and WINDY DAY: STORIES AND POEMS for J.B. Lippincott.

Caroline Bauer, with her husband and daughter, divides her time between Huntington Beach, California, and Chantilly, a town just outside Paris, France.

PETER SIS has illustrated a number of books for children, including AFTER GOOD-NIGHT by Monica Mayper and THE WHIPPING BOY by Sid Fleischman. He has also written and illustrated several of his own picture books, including RAINBOW RHINO, WAVING, and GOING UP. He was educated in London and Prague, where he made animated films. His work has been exhibited in Europe and the United States, and his drawings appear regularly in *The New York Times Book Review* and other publications. He now lives in New York City.